Reflections and Falling and Loving What's Lost

Reflections and Falling and Loving What's Lost
--
Ryan K. Allen

Ryan K. Allen
2020

© 2020 Ryan K. Allen.
All rights reserved.

Published by Ryan K. Allen, P.O. Box 7964, Chico, CA 95927.
Visit ryankallen.com.

ISBN 978-1-7356364-0-5

For Velma

Contents

Reflections

Something New	3
Unpublished Poems	4
Once upon a Time	5
Take Me Down	6
Shimmer	7
Across the Ice	8
Hello, Sunday	9
While the Bottles Still Last	11
There's a Film on the Sun	12
In the Light of the Moon	13
All That Shimmers	14
Every Piece of Me	16
The Sky Is Still Blue	17
I Will Always Follow You	18
Easy Chair	19
Sunset	20
On Willow Lake, in a Warm November	21
Me and My	22
Away from Me	23
How Time's Been Treating You	24
Awake	25
They Are Not Etched in Stone	26
Wolves	28
Neon	29
Sugar	30
Something to Believe	31
This Is Just Enough	32
Oscillation	33
Please-Give-Me-Relief	34
A Grinding, Constant Buzz	35
The Earth Is Swimming	36
23 Cents	37
These One Hundred Words	38
You Don't Have to Be Lonely	39
The Sea	40
Paperback	41
The Eras of You	42
Hole in My Jeans	43
Sour Apple	44
Fall into Some Understanding	45
Thoughts on Yesterday	47
Stacking Rocks	48

In the Sun	49
Hey, Sunshine	50
Arriving Calm	51
Summer Sun	52
Everything	53
As Far as I Fell	54

Falling

When Every Day Is Just a Day	57
At the Precipice	58
Dashing	59
The Not I Am	60
The Past Three Days	61
When No One's There to Hear Me Speak	62
Lake Spaulding	63
Flight	64
Sting	65
Dead Men	66
In the Night	67
Take Me Away	68
All It Is	69
29-Down	70
Overflow	71
Dragging Pt.2	72
Gibberish	73
	74
Only Me	75
Only a Surface	76
Spiral	77
Filling My Time	78
Loss of Time	79
Not Just a Waste of My Time	80
Overload	81
The Fall-Apart	82
Momentum	83
Curl	84
Falling Behind	85
Easy	86
The Void Pt.2	87
Volatile	88
The Void Pt.5	89
The Void Pt.6	90
Swing and Return	91
The Void Pt.14	92

```
Amongst the Trees........................................ 93
Butterfly................................................ 94
No One Left to Blame..................................... 95
I Fall Down.............................................. 96
Who I Am................................................. 97
Red...................................................... 98
Against the Rocks........................................ 99
Instead................................................. 100
I'm Falling Down........................................ 101
The Sun................................................. 102
```

Loving

```
Daring.................................................. 107
To Say What I Feel...................................... 108
Fall in Love............................................ 109
With You in My Brain.................................... 110
Green and Blue and Eyes................................. 111
She Said the Match Gods Sent Her Here................... 112
She Is a Face, So Far Away.............................. 113
Always.................................................. 114
Stars and Light......................................... 115
Where I Wanted Her...................................... 116
~~Save~~ Me............................................. 117
The One and Only You.................................... 118
Waiting for Tomorrow.................................... 119
Losing Your Touch....................................... 120
Shimmer, Don't Fade Away................................ 123
Say Goodbye............................................. 124
I Wouldn't Break........................................ 125
Missed.................................................. 126
Stranded and in Love.................................... 127
I Saw Your Face Out in the Pouring Rain................. 128
I Throw Myself Fully to the Notion of Love.............. 129
Saving.................................................. 130
Better Than Blue........................................ 131
Oh My Heart and My Love and My Dear..................... 132
Pitfalls and Promise.................................... 133
I Just Want Love........................................ 134
Prince Charming......................................... 135
Always There's You...................................... 136
Capital-B Be............................................ 137
She Is a Voice.......................................... 138
Closing Doors........................................... 139
Sundogs................................................. 140
Purple Days and Far Aways............................... 141
```

```
Stories of Hiking and Books about Flowers.............. 142
All I Wanted to Be..................................... 143
My Color Is Blue....................................... 144
Air.................................................... 145
You Have a Way......................................... 146
Far from Here.......................................... 147
Sunlight and Music and Color and Words................. 148
Two Hearts............................................. 149
When You're Out at Night, I Ignore the Stars........... 150
Sunset Pt.2............................................ 151
Everyone............................................... 152
Only Broken............................................ 153
The Void Pt.9.......................................... 154
What I Fear............................................ 155
You Weren't............................................ 156
All That I Knew........................................ 157
Fading................................................. 158
A Certain Kind of Love................................. 159
Happiness Pt.3......................................... 160
The City of the Setting Sun............................ 161
The Time That We Had................................... 162
All My Love............................................ 163
Long Ago............................................... 164
Habitual Tea........................................... 165
Yield to the Wind...................................... 166
All This Time.......................................... 167
Here's the Rain........................................ 168
```

                              Loss

```
3/6/20................................................. 171
Unaware................................................ 172
Deaths of Despair...................................... 173
All It Ever Will Be.................................... 174
Paths and Lines........................................ 175
Broken Circles......................................... 176
The Void Pt.10......................................... 177
In Blues............................................... 178
Phone It In............................................ 179
On Leaving............................................. 180
Just a Box............................................. 181
The Void Pt.11......................................... 182
When I Am Dying........................................ 183
The Void Pt.12......................................... 184
A Plastic Moon......................................... 185
```

```
Drying Lavender........................................ 186
As Soon as the Thunder Sounded......................... 187
Throw You Away......................................... 188
Ants................................................... 190
Facebook Marketing..................................... 191
Things Drawn Out by Mountain Sunsets................... 192
Listening to the Rain in the Dark...................... 193
An Unbearable Lightness................................ 194
6am.................................................... 195
She Wanted to Sing..................................... 196
Momentary Darknesses................................... 197
Winding and Open....................................... 198


Acknowledgements....................................... 199
```

Reflections

Something New

While I'm content
With something new
I'll push the things
I want to do

I'll push them back
I'll push away
And hour by hour
I push the day

The day will come
When I'm not here
I'll leave the weight
For light, I fear

So now, beset
With something new
I'll do the things
I want to do

And come the day
When I am gone
My plinth will be
This lexicon

Unpublished Poems

Thousands of unpublished poems
Are what I hope to leave behind
All those little pieces of me
But a fraction of my time

Once upon a Time

Once upon a time there was
A pattern in the airwave fuzz
Deep where there was nothing there
Someone felt the very air

Faces in the black and white
Life and love and day and night
The pattern held it all within
The red that someone stained it in

Who the faces really were
Where you and I and daylight blur
The world had seen it all in red
Until I saw in blue instead

And when that once in time I feel
The pattern that the air conceals
All life and love and day and night
Are everything but black and white

And deep within the very air
I'll live to breathe the nothing there
Where once upon a time there was
A pattern in the airwave fuzz

Take Me Down

Take me down in the cold of the river
Take me down to the bed underneath
Let me feel all the sand and the granite
The place where the water and earth ever meet

Shimmer

If I saw the difference between silver and gray
I wouldn't continue my shoes
One color shimmers and the other one bites
And I always forget how to choose

I say that I'm falling this dusty old road
Calling it lost and behind
But I'm only walking like everyone else
And everyone calls it design

To travel my past is mistaking around
Needing to fix my advance
All along following but never exist
Watching through aimless romance

Seeded the silver, I was alone in the night
All that shimmers will fade
Caught in the light, in no state to be told
Of every mistake to be made

You were the sadness etched in my walls
And all I knew was to spin
For once in my life, and silver beware
My image be damned, I gave in

I dreamed the salvation I dreamed within me
A mask in the stead of my face
In gratitude, care, dismissal, or hate
This shimmer is always my place

Across the Ice

As I set foot across the ice
I wonder just how thin it is
And if my foot breaks through
Will that water underneath be shallow
Or will it swallow me whole?

Hello, Sunday

Hello, Sunday
Please be gentle
Saturday was harsh
Both Friday and my love had gone away

And as I think of all the time
That has slipped me now
I realize that you are just a day

Hello, Tuesday
Take it slowly
So much in the air
But Monday's gone--it seems I've lost that time

And as I think of all the days
I spend within my head
I understand the place I fell behind

On Saturday, my love could only be a wrong
But it was not the only day I was not strong

So hello, Sunday
Please be gentle
The sun is rising slowly
Please don't shine your rays too harsh on me

And as I think of all the light
I've tried so hard to stop
I see it now, what I could never see

Hello, Thursday
How's the weather?
I think I'll stay inside
Wednesday's work no longer hides the rain

And as I think of every word
I curse within my head
I recognize I run away from pain

The days can only turn--we're only here or gone
But it's only to tomorrow where I'm drawn

So hello, Monday
Start me over
Let's begin again
And let the turn erase the time I hid

And as I think of all the time
Forever turning me
I often wonder all the good it did

While the Bottles Still Last

Casting out bottles to the foam of the sea
The messages entrusted but to cork and to glass
Recipients: any with nothing in hand
Reading of tales as if reading the last

The bottles will travel, cresting the waves
Stretching and cycling, thoughtless of time
The paper will brown through the film of the glass
Until sand and sea and bottle align

Align with an audience grasping the same
Apart, in comfort they wish to destroy
Falling on gospel lacking a context
Calling it meaning, lasting, and joy

Casting our bottles to the foam of the sea
Just words entombed under cork and in glass
Recipients: any wanting a path
Replacing their tales while the bottles still last

There's a Film on the Sun

There's a film on the sun
That separates what I know from what I see
For some it's a blanket or kaleidoscope lens
Distorting everything in reach
For me, it's just a film
I can see all the light, what shines beyond
While I'm trapped with what I know
And the two sides will never mix
I'll never know just what could be
If the film would only yield
All I see is the world through me
And from the world I remain concealed

In the Light of the Moon

I can't go out alone with the moon
The light I see reflecting a mess
Complement, yes, but currently waste
Nothing to me, but strong nonetheless

I can't go out, to stay in the dark
Comforting dress, this rotting away
Spending the day as well as the night
Delivers less, delivers okay

I can't go out in a night without dark
Spotlight my soul, too much to reveal
Something I feel, legitimate, true
Hardly a whole, and hardly ideal

I can't go out in the light of the moon
The face I see observing a mess
Intact, I guess, and only a part
Nothing to me, and strong nonetheless

All That Shimmers

Sitting down low in my bedroom, fifteen
Narrower view on living this thing
Pondering loneliness, silver, and wine
A rapid descent into filling my time

But creation, emotion, and me were the fill
Sadness the demon and struggles with will
The state I was in was given to me
In losing the love I wanted to be

As seventeen, nineteen, and twenty-one went
I watched from ahead the nothing I'd spent
What I had was all wrong from the start
The want that I made, the ache in my heart

What always went wrong, what I turned away
Was living the fear in burning the day
Turned from burning in blue to in red
The blue was still there, just buried and dead

The red was the demon--I knew it was mine
As I pondered loneliness, silver, and wine
But it's harder to learn without living it through
As I split from myself and struggled with you

With twenty-two passed and twenty-eight gone
Seven years, and blue all along
I forgot about silver, replaced it with gray
Only remembered that shimmers will fade

She was the sadness etched in my walls
I was the silver--I'd forgotten it all
All that shimmers will not fade away
Some things will last--some things will stay

I turned from burning in blue to in red
Could have been watching, but filling instead
Could have been decent, in living it through
Should have been decent and better to you

Everything now, I hope I'm aware
Burning in blue with nobody there
Fighting a place you've already been
Seeking the shimmer to never give in

Every Piece of Me

If I count
Each and every piece of me
Who I've been and who I'll be
Will I stand beside the grass
And all this world I see?

The Sky Is Still Blue

When I look back--this time I've been
I feel the ages in my skin
The time I saw the world in green
And how I felt at seventeen

The miles ago and years apart
The beating on, my beating heart
I'm ages from the me I was
But time will take the time it does

The ticking takes no note of me
Within the sway of every tree
We measure rainfall, votes, and sun
The weight of now in every one

When we look back--that time ago
We lose the weight we used to know
And think the ages make us new
I'm only me, and so are you

And so we are, and side by side
Believing now is where we're tied
Someone not in stone and clay
It must be different, every day

But as the time goes ticking on
And we look back on where we've gone
It's all the same, the things we do
The sky is still
   and just as blue

I Will Always Follow You

I know that I have always said
That I will always follow you
But now I know that that replaced
The things I should have been

Easy Chair

I once awoke in a period of color
And I wrote every word that came into my head
I wondered if living was different from dreaming
And so I gave up living for dreaming instead

I dreamed of a world just as shining as shallow
All the colors I wanted, I painted them there
In the glow of that dream, it all had a meaning
And it was too easy, falling into that chair

In the chair, I could sit and watch the horizon
Where the clouds and the sky met the earth and the grass
It all seemed to be held together by diamonds
After falling apart, I can see it was glass

There were times in the dream I put you in that chair
And pretended you saw all the same things as me
If living is anything different from dreaming
Then I showed you nothing that you wanted to see

Sunset

The sun doesn't set until you need its light to see
At least, this is what I've always noticed
And blamed it on everything--nature, the stars
Framed it in a conversation to you
Told you what to do, where I could lead
Or that we could wash along together

While the sun is shining, that's when I forget
Forget that I'm not writing to you
I was the one not ready to see--anything, everything
Framed it as something you needed to fix
Told you what you thought, what I had right
That we could wash away together

When the sun has fallen and I can't see you anymore
I tell you not to change your face to fit the scene
When you feel like me, you'll see--what? Anything?
Framed it as absolutely true
Told you anything and everything I see
And there never was a flow for us together

So wish on whatever you would like
A wishing well, an olive branch, the sun, or the moon
There are cycles where I wish there were not cycles
Framed in an apology to you
And what I told, I told in fear
There never was a sunset here

On Willow Lake, in a Warm November

The sun and the lake were a means to an end
To begin to talk about falling away
I wanted to fix everything into place
I thought the world of me for letting you in

I have always known there was something to trees
But not something so great as enlightenment
In everything green, there's a bit of my soul
And I leave it behind when I lie to you

A falling away was the end of my world
Those walls that I hated, the science there
Playing my god on a stage I constructed
While so far away were the lake and the sun

Describing to you what I saw from those halls
Through pinholes and darkness and paintings of fields
I called it all "perfection," "the best of me"
But I never questioned just what was my god

If letting you in is the best I can do
And I want to make peace with the falling away
I cannot forget what the lake is to all of us
And the sun and the trees
   and the something there is to it all

Me and My

To get a grip on anger me
To eschew love to anchor me
To live to live with dreaming my
To always know, believing my

Away from Me

I think I see you in the street
Where everybody is a blur
Their figures always incomplete
Photographs of who they were

And in turning to their faces
I find my eyes no longer see
Everybody in these places
Always walks away from me

I think I see you in my dreams
Where everybody is my mind
No matter how unfair, it seems
That I always fall behind

And in that shimmer where you glow
The place my eyes can never see
I say that you are all I know
Then you walk away from me

But in the day where I can see
Where everybody is their face
I find the emptiness in me
And this violent, angry chase

And in returning to that street
While looking out against the sea
I see that I was incomplete
That I ran away from me

How Time's Been Treating You

There are times I think I know
How time's been treating me
Where all the pieces fall
After everything I've seen

There are times throughout the night
When I should let it be
The times I think I know
Who I was at seventeen

There are times when I am great
And stand just where I am
I want to be it all
And I really think I can

There are times throughout the day
When I begin to damn
The person that I've been
And dismantle all my plans

There are times I think I know
How time's been treating you
And I will drop my dreams
To do what you want to do

But these times I think I know
I think are times I never knew
I think that I will never know
How time's been treating you

Awake

It all, alas, has come and gone
This time I spent before the dawn
The morning shines too bright to see
But all, at last, will come to be

They Are Not Etched in Stone

The easy, nameless din
Of lowering the sky
Blends the air with color
That's never set to dry

Eddies in the ether
The science of the hold
Gray the grays to silence
And fit the unfit mold

Travelers: the outside
Residents: a texture
Run the side horizon
Where yesterday they were

Explorers in the blood
With waterlogging heels
Mix their golden metals
And pour them into wheels

Tracks to carry water
Stain the very core
And lead the wheels away
From where they were before

She traced along apart
From anything they knew
The only one of her
Who could dream what she drew

Her sight was out for sale
A crushing in the snow
So delicate to her
That soon she wouldn't know

He invented angles
Defining air and sight
And reconstructed views
That only could be right

His hands amount a sum
A quenching in the flame
So strong within the walls
That keep that fire tame

Her silhouette is rust
His palette is the breeze
Their avenue a maze
Of stones around their knees

Monoliths but stunted
Various, together
Conquered by the color
The air, altogether

Years of din are washing
The texture from the dye
Erasing all the shape
The contour would imply

The force behind the blend
Erodes before they see
The palette of the stones
The mark they used to be

The dull, muted surface
Betrays a record face
Etched a false suggestion
Upon that perfect space

They do not stand in ruin
Though unseen and alone
The histories they see
They are not etched in stone

Though left-behind, apart
They are not etched in stone
Neglected flame unlit
A dryness never known

Disregard the faces
And harmonize the tone
Under tracks and color
They are not etched in stone

Wolves

I believe in wolves
And following gods
And marketing push
And living in pods

I believe progress
We aren't who we were
And singing along
And rapture in song

I believe in cars
And riding alone
We aren't who we were
And reading what's known

I believe in us
And bettering all
And breaking the wall
We aren't who we were

I believe in gods
And following gods
And marketing gods
And living as gods

We aren't who we were
Believing in wolves
And following wolves
We aren't who we were

Neon

The neon signs which light my god
That orange, red, and black facade
Those rounded, looming letters show
The fates I do not wish to know
Diseases highlight every glance
Cold, unmoving in their stance
Hung along my only path
Always there and true as math
The old commute which takes me past
A dooming program unsurpassed
Since I was young, I've held my breath
As I read "cancer," "mold," and "death"
One by one, those letters spell
And no one wants the things they sell
To turn away: to turn in vain
The barkers bark those words the same
Sitting hollow in that wall
A part of me, and that is all

Sugar

What's the worst that time can do?
I wonder from afar
Can sugar stay just as sweet
Lonely, in a jar?

The world is big, and I am not
Living in this town
Can sugar stay just as sweet
Even watered down?

It only seems I have a grasp
On who I was before
Can sugar stay just as sweet
When spilled upon the floor?

Every day, I ask myself
While falling to the ground
Can sugar stay just as sweet
When no one is around?

Something to Believe

Who do you think you are?
Do you think you have something to say?
Well, don't we all?
It's the price that we pay to feel loved
When all that holds our eyes
Is the swaying storm of photons in bloom

Why can't you see anymore?
Who do you think you're talking to?
It's only me
It's always only me, against the grain
Disturbing everything
That pattern shutting down what doesn't fit

Are you where you thought you'd be?
Are you satisfied with what you've done?
We're all young once
We all see that same sun in the sky
When did you look away?
When was that great, big blue just too much?

Is that it?
Too many miles, even for the speed of light?
Can you not slow down?
It's all a journey of bit by bit
The storm will slowly fade
If you can only handle bit by bit

Are you starting to see?
Can you navigate this mesh of dreams?
Do they blend together?
Each piece is better in the whole
And you are there
It's no mistake that you are there

I'm swimming in indigos, blues, and greens
It's up to you to decide what that means
I'm sitting here, seeing that I'm the same
Whatever keeps that fire aflame
Is fine with me
As long as I have something to believe

This Is Just Enough

Make a life
Not a comfort
Not a "this is just enough"

Oscillation

Up and down
That's all it is
Oscillation
Pop and fizz

Please-Give-Me-Relief

Is what I feel
A true belief
Or just a please-
Give-me-relief?

A Grinding, Constant Buzz

The grating ring of my apartment fridge
Is the soundtrack to my arrival

The Earth Is Swimming

Outside, the earth is swimming
It's all a ripple in cloth
Describing all that we wonder
And covering all that we've lost

Outside, the earth is swimming
In circles uneven and rough
Balking at all that we measure
And what we christen as luck

Outside, the earth is swimming
A portrait of brilliance and glare
Chronicling us at our greatest
And echoing us when we err

Outside, the earth is swimming
It's all a droplet of rain
Committing so very little
But building it all just the same

And outside, the earth is swimming
But inside is where I sit
Looking for a world with meaning
And I don't think this is it

23 Cents

Well, I have twenty-three cents in my pocket
If I was looking for a place to start
A place that isn't this city
A place that isn't my heart

Because this city is something too open
And yields an air I would like to avoid
To leave behind all my falling
And what I've yet to destroy

Because my heart is a fire or a relic
And at the moment is nothing so grand
Nothing deserving the spotlight
Nothing but water and sand

And these twenty-three cents aren't the answer
But they're something I am able to touch
Something that wets in the rainfall
But doesn't mean nearly so much

These One Hundred Words

These one hundred words will never be heard
Gone to the air like the wings of a bird
Emblazoned in ink on a page full of lines
A history told in symbols and signs

In symbols and signs, a telling of me
As only as ever I'd hoped I would be
Building a city in every word
A city whose story will never be heard

To never be heard, a fear that I know
A fear that remains in refusal to show
To show who I am, what I want, what I mean
To find in the world what I find in my dreams

What I find in my dreams will always be right
But always apart from the crisis of night
What I dream I desire--the desire a front
And logic may damn this emotional hunt

This emotional hunt is the search for it all
Through winter and springtime and summer and fall
Gone to the air as nothing, absurd
These one hundred words will never be heard

You Don't Have to Be Lonely

I saw your face, the way you walked into the room
I saw it all, as I see me
I know the day that falls apart by afternoon
Or earlier, eventually

I saw your eyes, the way they saw what wasn't there
That blue that bleeds the palette gone
And in the cold of everything you'd ever care
You sleep so you will never yawn

    But you don't have to be lonely
    It's what I'm feeling too
    And while it's cold inside this place
    It's warm outside with you

And what I saw was that familiar midnight blue
There's just no one who feels exactly like you do

The Sea

The sea has always felt like it was something grand
A little bit of myth where the water meets the land
Every time I'm there, I'm a mirror of the tide
And I know I live my life where sand and wave collide

Paperback

I've always loved a paperback
The way it wears along with me

The Eras of You

The eras of you that you define
As strokes of music and books in time
Those words, that piece of who you are
So near to you, to me so far
Those words, that tether in between
What I see and what you've seen
It's all of you, as I have mine
Those strokes of music and books in time

Hole in My Jeans

As time and friction work to wear this threadbare spot I see
I think of how the time and friction work to wear on me
The thinning of these cotton strands, so strong until they break
Continues on with every step and every day I take
My body rails against the cold this hole is letting in
A perfect imitation of defenselessness I've been
As I stand here, prepared to buy a brand new pair of jeans
I think of all the walls I've built and what this shelter means
As I remember every step and every day you gave
I think of all the walls I've built and tried so hard to save

Sour Apple

I used to think sometimes that people were just bad
But I'm not sure that I believe that anymore
Because a lot of times the world can break you down
And as much as you may try, you just can't break the world

Fall into Some Understanding

I guess I'd always hoped I would simply fall
Into some understanding of the world
Into some kind of peace

I think it *can* happen that way
If everything lines up how you always hoped it would
But mostly you don't get anywhere on hope alone

You don't fall into understanding
You work and you try and you build that understanding
You and no one else

You don't fall into peace of mind
You fall into pits and darkness
Steered by everyone, anyone but you

You don't fall from what's behind
You stand upon it, darkness and all
Your plinth will hold, but you still have to stand

A falling is a lack of effort
Letting the sway of the universe push you where it wants
Against rocks and trees, scraping and sliding

Events will occur which are out of your control
You may lose a bit of yourself
Continue to stand

You will be told who you are and what to believe
And how small is the value you bring
Continue to stand

The world will batter you until you fall
Entropy comes for even the most steadfast of feet
Don't help it by just giving way

No one can help you, but you are not helpless
Your plinth always grows as the clock ticks away
Even if you cannot see, look!

You won't always see, but look!
Because if you never look, you will never see
And if you never try, never build, never stand

You'll never find that understanding
You'll never get that peace of mind
You will be consumed by what's behind and who you've fallen
  down to be

       I have not fallen
       Into some understanding of the world
       Though I have fallen
       If I've done anything at all, I've fallen

       And if I've done anything at all
       I've gained that understanding
       I'm finding a peace of mind
       Bit by bit by agonizing bit, I stand

       And I smile
       Just to think of it

You cannot demand a shape from the world
Not by heat or by coaxing or mold
You can only control that plinth and your feet
And value the ground that you hold

Thoughts on Yesterday

As I sit at this table where my time only bleeds
And the light filters in off the new springtime leaves
The air strikes a balance, inside and without
And for just this one time, I know what life is about

My grandmother's table, her cloth, and her chairs
Are the weight handed down where only lightness was there
The pieces we saved when the cycle was broken
And here I sit, on every word ever spoken

At the coming of spring, all this green is the truth
It seems like a cycle that won't break like we do
As we sit here at tables, in chairs we forgot
Billions of cycles who think we are not

When does the air in a life gain a weight
If the light on this table is a nature that's fake?
These words that I feel are nothing close to that green
And I never exist outside of this screen

But outside, the earth, in its brilliance of color
Cascades through my window and creates yet another
A color that travels but once, in my place
A chance for the world to remember this face

It was not a decision, but it's entirely mine
This wild fascination with the passage of time
What's wasted, what's left, and how much I care
For my life to be passed in a table and chairs

The air in a lifetime spans the distance between
A table and chairs and the lightness of being
A world in balance, inside and without
As I sit at this table, I know what life is about

Stacking Rocks

In stacking rocks within this field
I aim to show the thoughts I wield
And mitigate destruction of
What binds us to the sky above

In the Sun

There's a place that I go to be whole
When I can't feel a thing
When I'm losing control
In the sun, in the sun, in the sun

Hey, Sunshine

Where I was young, I held you ever
Golden on my skin
I didn't know you'd always made
The state that I was in

In every ray that I ignored
There shone a bit of me
And now the happiness I was
Is just a memory

November snow and April rain
Are everything around
They beat my skin and wash away
The gold into the ground

I cannot paint that shine in place
That light unique to you
And so I settle in the shade
And paint my fire blue

Arriving Calm

Looking past this field of flowers
A sense of calm comes over me
I can feel the sunshine coming
Falling down so I can see

Summer Sun

The autumn rain has not begun
Yet I await the summer sun
The wind does not admit a chill
Yet I await the summer still
The summer, when I will exist
The blazing sun the winter missed
But if I stay just who I've been
Then I'll await the sun again

Everything

I dream about it
Everything
Nothing is ever
What it seem

I live in color
Blue and green
I dream in rapid
Everything

The spin and ripple
What I mean
I want a little
Everything

I walk in silent
Everything
I drink of violent
Isolene

I'm gone and lost in
Everything
In lost the meaning
Movie scene

Without the follows
Dream a dream
Without the ending
Everything

As Far as I Fell

I've arrived out of darkness
Culled from the well
I never hit bottom
As far as I fell

Falling

When Every Day Is Just a Day

I look forward to the day
When every day is just a day
And not this crisis I have always known

At the Precipice

I'm at the precipice of *giving up*
Of getting *back on track*
Of losing all the *greatness* here

    Of fading back to black

Dashing

Sometimes I think about numbers
And how many I think it will take
Until I dash all my dreams on the rocks
Until I fall down and break

The Not I Am

My self-imposed
My lines and goals
They stifle all I am

I shy away
I waste the day
And fear the not I am

The Past Three Days

I've slept so much the past three days
For failing having tried
When nothing's left of living here
Then dreaming's where I'll hide

When No One's There to Hear Me Speak

When no one's there to hear me speak
I'll shout until my will is weak
While no one's there to hear me say
I don't deserve it anyway

When no one's there to hear me cry
I'll shout until my voice is dry
While no one's there to hear me scream
I'm not the confidence I seem

When no one's there to see me fall
I'll shout until I lose it all
While no one's there to see me great
It's me, and only me, I hate

When no one's there to help me stand
I'll shout until I'm only sand
While no one's there to help me be
Anyone but only me

When no one's there to hear me speak
I'll shout until my will is weak
While no one's there to hear me say
I'll keep on shouting anyway

Lake Spaulding

I lyse my hand, my psyche split
A cruel divide, an eon pit
In sober din, leftover place
I don't belong--I'm not my face

The price of string to shape my hold
The price to stay the risk of cold
At dawn I pay--my troubles seep
I lie alone--I never sleep

Flight

The devil's in, the lion's gone
My heart is beating, beating on
I check it once--say I'm wrong?
I check again, and check along

The beat, the drum, the dark, the night
I will not rest without a fight
The paper's gone, electrons in
I feel the phone against my skin

Quell me now--just settle me!
There is no beast I have to flee
Just spots and hum and chime and glow
I wish I could, but I don't know...

Sting

While morning rises, nighttime falls
And in the night, those words will call
The ones that sing before they're said
The ones that sting
The ones that spread

Dead Men

Here's what I know:
That dead men get down
They're sleeping away
Their days in the ground

Here's what I know:
That strong men grow old
They sweat in the heat
And shiver in cold

Here's what I am:
I'm living and down
Burning in flame
In water and drowned

Here's what I am
After all I've been told:
I'm down and I'm strong
I'm dead and I'm old

In the Night

It's in the night--the shades are drawn
For several hours, I've been gone
I lyse my hand, if in my mind
The perfect me is left behind

Of crises drawn and breaking split
I bleed in time to think of it
I need to end--I need to rest
I hope to me I did my best

Take Me Away

The moon is burning red tonight
And shining down on me
All I asked for was some light
So that I could see

I wanted guidance, just to know
That all would be okay
But all the fire burning here
Has taken me away

All It Is

I'm just tired
That is all
I want to sleep
That is all

I shouldn't think
I'll only spin
I shouldn't think
The state I'm in

I want a lot
I want it all
I need to sleep
That is all

29-Down

Droplets of blood, sometimes:
What it takes to fit in

Overflow

So much weight was pressed upon me
With such potential down below
As the evening sought to fill me
I sought an edge to overflow

Dragging Pt.2

I have no goals
I lost the reason I--
Dragging my life away
I am not fine

Gibberish

Bang-a-lang, it's gibberish day
Ding-a-ling-lang-a-hey-de-hey-day
What the hell is this? I'm avoiding a fight
Call my companion "crisis," "the night"

This page intentionally left blank

Only Me

From my nowhere, it's just me
Sabotaging all of me
Ending every sentence "me"
All along and only me

Only a Surface

It's all so fragile
What makes us whole
Call it a neuron
Or call it a soul

All of this falling
Just entropy, plain
Only a surface
Keeps each of us sane

Spiral

I've got to get a grip on my spiral
Just what sends me down to my depths
Because I'm wasting my life
Concerned about whether or not I'm wasting my life

Filling My Time

I'm filling my time
And filling my time
And filling my time
And filling my time

Loss of Time

I get behind, but I don't mind
No one holds me to my mind
Lazy rhymes and loss of time
And loss of time and loss of time

Not Just a Waste of My Time

I put a lot on my plate
But it's never enough
Never enough to ensure

That I stay satisfied
That I'm not just a waste
Not just a waste of my time

Overload

This overload is just the same
As any drug upon my brain
I melt into the ether here
That much I know. That much is clear.

The Fall-Apart

I fucked it up, my momentum
I'm all my mood and all alone
Is who I am what I invented?
This fall-apart is all I've known

Momentum

My momentum is gone
I'm no longer strong
I'm sleeping too much
I wonder what's wrong

I know that it's me
It's just something inside
I need outside force
To keep me alive

I've thought about passion
To follow a dream
But passion won't feed me
I'm just a machine

Back among everything
I'd love to need you
But it's just an idea
That I'd love to be true

As everything falls
There's only the ground
How much of me
Is worth keeping around?

I just need a push
A push and a shove
It has to be me
I just wish it were love

I just need a push
To get me to go
My momentum is gone
That's what I know

Curl

Such an award I wish I could gain
As everyone knowing and singing my name
But everything--*everything*--all is in vain
As I curl away, and the time does the same

Falling Behind

I may have stopped progress
Mistaking my mind
Thinking of thinking
But falling behind

Easy

Garden variety
I'm nothing so great
Easy to lie to me
I'm easy to hate

The Void Pt.2

I scream that void
That void I scream
It screams until
I shout my dreams
My dreams they shout
Out, to the night
That night, that crisis
Lack of light
That light, that glow
That diamond there
I scream the diamond
"I don't care"
At last, the care
And what it seems
I scream that void
That void I scream

Volatile

Alas, alas, the time, the sun
Where have all the children run?
Dread befalls me--inner hum
Shrugs the rhythm, tears the drum

The Void Pt.5

I've got to write something
The void is returning
The sinking is coming
And I'm all alone

The Void Pt.6

Somewhere along the line
I lost my honesty
And I am in danger now
Of losing my intention

I'm in full panic
And that's no way to live
But I don't know how
To live any other way

Am I unraveling?
Is my mind in full spiral?
Can I gain some purchase
As I flail wildly in the void?

I don't know
And I always come back around
To "I don't know"
And that's my sticking point

All my life I've had to know
And dropped it all if I didn't
And what do I have to show for it?
Not happiness. Not in the least.

So, fuck it
Fuck the unraveling
I'm me and only me
And fuck the spiral and the purchase

I am the void
This void I scream
And as the void
I only dream
But what are we
But inner thoughts?
So here I drop
All that I'm not

Swing and Return

I'm falling apart
I'm changing around
The swing and return
Of season and sound

The Void Pt.14

And still I worry
When no one's sitting here but me
Obsessing over breaking free
Collapsing in a flower bed
And calling color "void" instead

Amongst the Trees

I walk amongst the trees
Adorned with fading green
And I whisper to the leaves
"You will fall just like me"

Butterfly

I am caught underneath
A mosaic of blues
But I wish that I shone
Under happier hues
And I wish that my touch
Didn't float on the air
I just float on the air
   I just float on the air

No One Left to Blame

It wasn't the job that was suffocating me
And once that proclaimed evil had been laid to rest
The world suffered as it always had

With no one left to blame
The surface had never seemed so out of reach
And it was all that I could do
Just to wash up coughing on the beach

I Fall Down

I
Fall
Down

Down
    Down
        Down

Who I Am

This is just who I am
And it sucks
And it's great
And I'm broken in two

Red

I cannot slip
Or I paint it all red
With these colorful lichens
That grow in my head

I slip and I skin
My knee on the rocks
And the red of my blood
Meets the red of that pox

And I cover it all
All the blue that I love
The deep of the sea
And the light from above

As I sink down into
The microbial mud
A perfect reflection
Of weakness I was

And as I sink down
Into weakness I am
I try to remember
The water and sand

The water and sand
That bit of divine
A piece of it all
A piece that is mine

And I watch all the red
As I wash it away
And I thank everything
That I made it today

Against the Rocks

I'm getting a handle on
What makes me slip away
The stressors and the hurdles
That make me dash the day

Instead

All the time, I only want
To fold in on myself
And sometimes I fold, but other times
I breathe the air instead

And while I breathe, I think of all
This mess I make my head

And while I breathe, I see how small
Is all this mess instead

I'm Falling Down

I constantly describe myself as *falling down*
As if that action could continue forever
As if there's no slam into another body
And the direction is always an absolute

In an instant, that single phrase is all I am
I'm stuck in the endless process of falling down
Waiting for the landing to regain my control
Mired in the unbroken inaction of waiting

If I ever really fall, there is a landing
Whether it's a crash or a settling, it's there
But somehow I seem to miss those stretches of calm
Those periods of stillness between the falling

And by design there is only one way to fall
Down into the sadness that wasn't there before
Down into everything that I don't want to be
Yet into all that I have chosen as my path

And that's it, isn't it? That I've chosen this course
From that instant I described myself as falling
I pushed myself and denied myself a landing
And I think I've always known I'm the one to blame

That knowledge doesn't make it feel much easier
The designation is so often subconscious
But I am beginning to see what starts the fall
And what keeps me spiraling forever downward

The catalyst is almost always a letdown
I don't build my hopes to withstand a coming storm
And if I see that storm, I never start to hope
And without a perfect outcome, it's all a waste

Then I start fueling the spiral with distraction
But it's less a fueling than a turning away
If I can't think about it, then I'll never hurt
But that's not true. I'll always find a way to hurt

And the one thing that has always stopped my falling
Is having someone here who I could love
But just as easily as love can pull me up
It can shove me down even further than before

And so my emotions hinge on the external
I cannot control the falling inside of me
I've always thought that one day I'd control myself
But maybe I just need to let me be

And I don't feel like I've made a breakthrough
Because I don't think that life works that way
It may end up the way it always has
And if it does, I think I'll be okay

The Sun

I do not fall
I'm not undone
I will be great
I am the sun

Loving

Daring

And so I'll venture with my heart
Endure the times I fall apart
Dare to think it might come true
And dare to think it may be you

To Say What I Feel

It's hard for me
To say what I feel
To say what I should
To someone who's real

I know I should
Just open my heart
But opening up
Would tear me apart

So listen now
And read from my eyes
And read what I write
I never write lies

Fall in Love

The leaves will change to fall in love
The winter rain, the sky in love
The spring will carry green in love
The heat, the summer sun in love

    And every day
      I fall in love with you

With You in My Brain

Outside my window or inside my mind
I fall in love with you all the time
Outside you're pretty--inside's the same
I'm falling over with you in my brain

Green and Blue and Eyes

That everywhere green in the trees and the grass
The deepening blue of the water and sky
The infinite beauty of it all, all along
Is all along nothing in a world with your eyes

She Said the Match Gods Sent Her Here

Avoiding time enough to fear
She said the match gods sent her here
I asked of all potential views
She said the match--she didn't choose

I wanted insight to my fate
The strained election of my state
In lieu, perhaps, is someone dear
She said the match gods sent her here

She Is a Face, So Far Away

She is a face, so far away
My eyes are blue--my spirits gray
I'll see her soon, but not today
She is a face, so far away

She is her eyes that shine like stars
They cut right through this world of cars
We're far apart, with eyes like ours
She is her eyes that shine like stars

She is her soul, so full of care
The future rests, and soundly, there
She's only good, and this I swear
She is her soul, so full of care

She is a face, so far away
I see it now, and I'm okay
I'll see her soon, but not today
She is a face, so far away

Always

I hope that you don't drag me down
I just can't shake the thought
And so I'll drag myself away
Consumed by what you're not

Stars and Light

The sparkle there that brought me down
Last time I could not be found
I called it stars and called it light
An E to cut away the night

And now I name the stars again
And say I recognize the end
But everything is something new
I'll always wrap myself in you

Where I Wanted Her

A newly opened book to write
A later-than-I-wanted night
A maybe, could-be, if-it-were
And nothing where I wanted her

~~Save~~ Me

You left me there
When I needed you
You walked away
I wasn't fine

The One and Only You

I lost a bit of me
And there's nothing you can do
Because the one that I have lost
Is the one and only you

The one and only you
Who I wanted just so bad
To be that bit of myth
That perhaps I never had

Waiting for Tomorrow

I stared out the window, face on the glass
Waiting for tomorrow and the next day to pass
I wanted your love, I wanted you back
There was a lot about me that I couldn't unpack

Losing Your Touch

The day is black
The day, today
My heart, it beats
On, anyway

I think I can
I think I see
What is your mind
Your mind to me

The trouble here
The bliss I know
It's not this place
This time ago

The light is cast
The shadow, clear
You hide behind
The shadow here

Where I believe
It all went right
Where I see stars
You see the night

I must have known
That aimless song
I think I knew
It all along

What breaks the day
What breaks it down
This obstacle
Is all around

And when you sing
The sadness on
This breaking down
Is never gone

The someone here
Was someone you
I grew to love
That sky of blue

I'm in the air
In me this hole
I feel the air
Within my soul

In living now
The earth may shake
In dreaming how
My world will break

I dream about
I dream it all
My goal has been
To always fall

I'm by the sea
Familiar place
The place where I
Can't see my face

The way I walk
I'm walking blind
And tethered here
You walk in kind

The steps we were
Escape us now
But shape it all
It all, somehow

There's nothing left
I'm thinking, just--
The only thing
That's left is trust

--

There's a frequency turning into day after day
When day after day is too much
And "Don't you forget me" is all I can say
When I feel that I'm losing your touch

Shimmer, Don't Fade Away

I dream. Nothing new.
Holding on. And on to you.
Losing trust. What I feel.
What I dream. I dream it real.

I want. Not a thought.
Silver you. And I am not.
Damning form. Carving lines.
Without today. I will be fine.

I love. Nothing there.
Always light. To say I care.
Easier. Just to fear.
Just to think. In honey, here.

I lose. Not a thing.
Secretly. It's everything.
Built-up. Well-behaved.
Holding on. Cannot be saved.

I mean. Nothing more.
Seeing on. I see before.
And I mean. What I say.
Shimmer, please. Don't fade away.

Say Goodbye

All I wanted was for you to love me too
And I hung onto that for much too long
I steamrolled this city to make room for you
But in beating myself down, I was wrong

Every time I say goodbye

I Wouldn't Break

What's it like to be hit by a bus?
To run headlong into a closed door?
To feel compelled to run forever?
To be sure all life is a snowstorm?

What's it like to be hit by the sun?

I should know, the way I threw myself
Blindly to the mercy of young love

Oh, and I said that I wouldn't break
I said that you could put me through hell
And I wouldn't break

But I thank you that you did not
My own head was hell enough for me

And that bus--that bus was jealousy
The door was the edge of my comfort
I ran so fast away from myself
All I felt inside was that snowstorm

But I always knew you were the sun
And that's what broke me in the end

Missed

I never saw your eyes that way
I said I did, but in the gray
Of begging you to, please, just stay
I would have said it all

I said I heard your voice at night
And through the rain, it was the light
But sound is only sound, not sight
I missed my mark on that

And now I see I saw your smile
Not inside out, but juvenile
A surface, a reflection, while
I knew not even me

I held your hand and held your kiss
For far too long, I called it bliss
All I'm trying to say is this
I missed you even so

Stranded and in Love

I'm a human
I'm an artist
I'm unhinging
I'm a god

I believe it
I can see it
I am empty
And in love

I'm a thinker
I'm a target
I'm revolting
I'm a lot

I employ me
I destroy me
I am sliding
And in love

I'm a person
I'm an artist
I'm insensate
I'm a god

I'm a human
I'm a lover
I am stranded
And in love

I Saw Your Face Out in the Pouring Rain

I saw your face out in the pouring rain
Where grays and blues cut the black away
I'm unsure now if it was sweet or pain
But rain has always felt that way

I Throw Myself Fully to the Notion of Love

I'm caught so deeply in anything that gives me pleasure
I throw myself fully to the notion of love
My life is a constant quest to find meaning
And I'm always swept too far out to sea
Out to that sea, that sea of red
Caught so deeply I just waste away
And love is the force I always thought would rescue me
Rescue me
It's a giving-up to say it, to read it here
To throw myself to the whims of the outside
To look myself in the eyes and finally say
That swim is a bitch
And I think I should not throw away my salvation
I need to hold the line that pulls me back
But is that a defensiveness? A strangulation?
Should I lend the line only to love?
What else might save me?

--

My life is a constant quest for salvation
I throw myself fully to the notion of love

Saving

And as you go to save the world
To right the evils being hurled
Remember all that gets you through
And let the world go saving you

Better Than Blue

The glow is gone
I'm all-over dim
The body is strong
But feeling is thin

I wish for love
As strong as the night
My feeling is mud
It's me that I fight

I know not who
Or what she could be
But better than blue
And better for me

Oh My Heart and My Love and My Dear

My heart is the air and the water and sand
My love is the place where the sea meets the land
And you are the rocks that continue to stand
By the splintering wood of the pier

My heart is this chair, where I sit and I hope
My love is this bed that I'm using to cope
And you are the dream, the invisible rope
To establish the time of the year

My heart is a cycle of breaking routine
My love is a season of purple and green
And you are the day and the hours between
That make violence and weight disappear

My heart is the way of the stars in the sky
My love is the way that I don't say goodbye
And you are the way that you breathe when you cry
Oh my heart and my love and my dear

Pitfalls and Promise

Life is a plane of pitfalls and promise
A constant struggle of meeting our eyes
What does it mean that you're looking for love?
What if love can't get me to rise?

I Just Want Love

In this cold around my bones
In this game we play with phones
I just want love
I just want love
I just want love

Prince Charming

I am not your Prince Charming
I am nobody's "come save me from this"
But I'll listen when you speak
And I'll hang on just how it is that you exist

Always There's You

Always there's you
You sound like an angel
You spin me around
And shine on the night

Always there's you
You look like I'm dreaming
You make me a hero
When nothing is right

Always there's you
You're everything lovely
You turn me to stone
And give to me flight

Always there's you
Could I be so lucky
To hear all your thoughts
And shine in your light?

Capital-B Be

Everything--the air, the trees
The smell of water on the breeze
I see my life, and all I know
Will melt into the ground below

So let it melt and melt with me
When everything is all we see
In all the air, in every tree
We see the mold, that way to Be

She Is a Voice

She is a voice, out from the dark
That freezing void, forever stark
She sings her words, her words the sun
She holds me here with every one

Closing Doors

As I go closing doors in my apartment
To keep the heat from rooms with no one there
I think of all the doors I close inside my head
And think that I should let you in instead

Sundogs

The rain fell down
It always has
Can never be undone
But blazing through
That streaking blue
A circle 'round the sun

Purple Days and Far Aways

The green and yellow and black and blue
The stages of healing inside of you
The bruise, that purple of the day
Dramatic as it is, you say
Is what you've brought here to me
The color you and I can see
And come, if ever, the day we are
How beautiful that purple scar

Stories of Hiking and Books about Flowers

I dare not think what might have been
If I'd not messaged you again
The last few weeks have been the sun
And every day the greatest one

All I Wanted to Be

I had a hard time looking at you
There was so much light in the air
Your voice fell down like summer rainfall
And all I wanted to be was there

My Color Is Blue

As I thought about her, she was the color of canyons
And the clay and the earth of the riverbed
And while the rain fell down, as it always will
It was a dream that I thought about her instead

Air

All I've learned about the air
Is how it holds the blue we know
And if we're never far apart
The blue will never show

You Have a Way

You have a way that you smile when you think
A way that you tilt your head to the side
When you ask me if I know what you mean
And I know what you mean, but I don't know who you are
And I'm wishing that someday I would
That someday you'll tilt your head to the side
And say nothing
   but be understood

Far from Here

I never was so far away
So far away from here
As when, for her, I turned aside
The silver of my mirror

Sunlight and Music and Color and Words

A circle 'round the sun is nothing
The color of the earth not much
When set against her only smile
And the hold-me-ever of her touch

--

Sometimes she defies description
Though I may try to pin her down
We sometimes must forego the why
Enjoy the music for the sound

--

This circle 'round my heart is now
Where I will spend my days
In coloring the world around
I hope this color stays

In circling my heart in song
I hope to count the ways

--

If I've ever written a single word
It all becomes a blur
Every single word I've written
It all has led to her

Two Hearts

And through the stream of hearts and years
The grip of fear and sting of tears
We fight that ever current for
The words we long to hear

If never it should come, that day
Two hearts within that river's way
I dare not hesitate and lose
The words I want to say

When You're Out at Night, I Ignore the Stars

"Nothing shines as bright as you"
Is old and worn, but still the truth
In the darkness over me
It's you, and only you, I see

Sunset Pt.2

In any good there is to me
The end is all that I can see
And so I make the end appear
There's only ever sunset here

Everyone

The night was young
And there I was
Curled into a ball

As much as I
Had seen the end
It still hurt after all

If I had not
Those years ago
Decided not to drink

I would have met
Oblivion
And not have stopped to think

In everyone
I love, I see
The only thing I know

In everyone
I love who leaves
It's everything that goes

Only Broken

My heart is only broken
But I'm lying on the floor
Lamenting how another
Slipped away just like before

My heart is only broken
And I'm nothing else but sand
And love is just like water
As it falls right through my hands

My heart is only broken
And you're only everything
A world of lights and colors
That I'll never get to sing

My heart is only broken
And it doesn't have a clue
That just what you meant to me
Well, I never meant to you

My heart is only broken
Scattered pieces in the air
The bits of you escaping
And I want to leave them there

The Void Pt.9

I set my mind on removing air
To find the void that's everywhere
Everywhere that I am not
I scream that void
        I scream a lot

I set my mind on fading gray
To see if you will fade away
Anywhere that I am not
At last, the care
        I care a lot

What I Fear

The burn is still within my heart
At night I always fall apart
Spinning now without you here
This is it
   is what I fear

You Weren't

You weren't just a bed
You weren't just a light
You weren't just a warmth
In a world of night

You weren't just your eyes
You weren't just a face
You weren't just a soul
In the nothing of space

You weren't just a story
You weren't just an act
You weren't a retelling
Leaving nothing intact

You weren't an idea
But you weren't only you
You weren't just another
Love to live through

You were a dream coming true

All That I Knew

I sat in the darkness
Remembering you
And the days when your face
Was all that I knew

Fading

The wind cuts through the warming here
This undecided time of year
Reminds us that it's not yet spring
But nothing stops--that's the thing

I never thought the spring would come
Without you here, without the sun
Without a gold to cut this blue
This midnight color bleeding through

This stinging cold against my cheek
Is all I wanted, all I seek
To steal me from the warming day
I beg this fading wind to stay

As time goes by, I feel afraid
Of just how much of love can fade
As time goes by, I fade from you
And that's the thing--you're fading too

A Certain Kind of Love

I said there wasn't any love
That I was merely almost there
While I was not too long removed
From yielding fully to despair

But time has passed, and still I write
And think about you in the night
If only trace upon the air
A certain kind of love was there

Happiness Pt.3

Happiness is interesting
As memories of her flash through my mind
When will they be gone?
Because they *will* be gone

That was not a happiness I was holding onto
It was another placeholder in a lifetime of placeholders
And I'm finally feeling like I can shed the placeholders
And I think I'm done grasping madly for her

But not done enough that I still wouldn't fall
Madly in love with her
Given the chance

Happiness is a letting go

The City of the Setting Sun

I thought the sun had set
I thought my time was gone
I thought no love was here
And I was moving on

I let the darkness in
I let the future go
I let the ceiling fall
And I stayed down below

And while the world was dark
I heard a sound I knew
It was the breaking waves
I followed them to you

While you were here I saw
And felt the time I had
The love I thought I'd lost
For that, I'm only glad

And though you had to go
You brought me to the sea
And I'll forever live
With you as part of me

--

So run through the city of the setting sun
Run to the edge of the sea
I hope that you don't run too long
But I hope that you run free

The Time That We Had

As I read all the books
The books that she's read
I think of the mess
That she's made my head

But not only a mess
It's beautiful too
These books that I read
The things that I do

The things that I do
With my head out of spin
The colors I see
The state that I'm in

The mess is beautiful
Even if I'm sad
Because the time that we spent
Was the time that we had

All My Love

I cannot capture all my love
In words upon a screen
In notes within a song
In colors in a dream

I capture all my love within
Your voice upon the air
Our fingers when we touch
In every breath we share

I capture just to hold that love
When you are not around
In even just that bit of love
I can nearly drown

Long Ago

Although I saw her here today
We lost her long ago

--

That's all I could think to write
As your grandmother forgot who she was
And half of the words were yours

I don't know which was stronger
The sorrow I felt
Or my want to feel sorrow

Just as I don't know
If it was love that I felt
Or my want to feel loved

And there may be no fault
But I'm sorry for that
And I'm sorry that our paths have split

--

And I can't help thinking that this is it
These wants and loves that make a life
And all these things
   that we can't think to write

Habitual Tea

Just like I'm falling further from you
I think I'm becoming myself

Yield to the Wind

When nothing is left
Which I must debate
I yield to the wind
I leave it to fate

The price of a plan
Is ticking me down
So yield to the wind
From city to town

I hunger for sleep
And yearn for the truth
I yield to the wind
The compass of youth

My words have run dry
No will to pretend
I yield to the wind
I'll love in the end

All This Time

Strange times
And hearts beat on
Until those times
Those times are gone

Here's The Rain

Here's the rain
I love that sound
Things imploded
I eroded
And all my tears came down

Loss

3/6/20

Unaware

Life goes on
Until it doesn't
We run ourselves
We leave behind

Deaths of Despair

Blockbuster movies and deaths of despair
And isn't it nice, this breeze in the air?
Among stranded belongings and paintings of trees
There are no words for the mark that it leaves

"Isn't it awful?" and, "How could it be?"
And, "Where can we get a breakfast for free?"
And sometimes it sucks, but the trade-off is fair
Blockbuster movies for deaths of despair

All It Ever Will Be

It's a new day
It's a new day
It's a new day
Day
Day
Day
And that's it
That's all it is
That's all it ever was
And all it ever will be

Paths and Lines

Life
And all it brings
Love and sorrow
Everything

Broken Circles

To fall back into the past
And live out life in that place
Would mean that I'd no longer exist
But I'd always remember her face

The Void Pt.10

I turned away
This part of me
This window pane
This balcony

I chose instead
This dull, this void
This emptiness
That I enjoyed

Alone, in pain
But secretly
I even kept
The shade from me

But I exist
I cannot stay
Devoid of sight
And turned away

But turned against
The noise and fear
A substance in
The lightness here

A plinth to hold
What might be gone
The weight where you
Continue on

In Blues

This is where I live
And this is where I lose
In love and life and loss and grief
I dream this home in blues

Phone It In

I'll phone it in tonight
Hope you don't mind
You're all I've got right here, right now
But nothing's left of me

On Leaving

I'm not quite past the mourning here
I see your message on my phone
And all I want to do right now
Is leave you all alone

Just a Box

With life distilled to just a box
We're left with what refused to go
The part that doesn't feel
It's everything you didn't want
And still it doesn't leave
With all the color burned away
It's hard to think it's real
A box, a *box*, it's just a box
I can't believe it's real

The Void Pt.11

One day at a time
I claw my way back
From my love and heartache and grief
And I ask, once again
What life do I want?
But the void isn't screaming relief

When I Am Dying

As sirens blare
And proteins fold
Am I just doing
What I'm told?

As roads are paved
And blood cells fight
Am I just daylight?
Am I night?

In evening smog
In nicotine
When I am dying
Will I dream?

In crisp A/C
In dopamine
When I am dying
Will I scream?

The Void Pt.12

A tangled mess
Of gray and black
A string I'm never
Getting back
Suspended in
This void in me
Hardly there
And hard to see
Rules my daylight
Ticks my night
And makes this nothing
Feel alright

How long until
This tangled mess
Is all I see
When I undress?

How long until
This void in me
Is all I see?
   Is all I see?

Is all I see
This nothing here?
It's what you saw
Is what I fear.

A Plastic Moon

I see the moon--the moon is bare
It leaves me clear and too aware
A tiny speck, a sea of black
Are what I have and what I lack

The ache, the cold, the dark, the night
I build a sky to block the light
And in the vacuum I erase
A plastic moon will take its place

Beneath the artificial glow
A dancing I presume to know
I bask until I cannot bear
The very fabric of the air

And in the din to which I'm drawn
That never-silent never-dawn
A thread unravels from the cloth
A plastic moon to steer the moth

The even circles of my flight
Are deep enough to mark the night
And in this dimming I'd be glad
For just that tiny speck I had

And there's the moon--the moon is bare
It's what I lack--it's always there
A thread unravels from the thought

    A plastic moon to tie the knot

Drying Lavender

Someone's mother died
And like the flowers wilt
Here on this table
We go about forgetting

As Soon as the Thunder Sounded

As soon as the thunder sounded
It started raining so hard
I smiled at how much I loved that sound
The landing droplets splashed a fine spray
Through the window screen onto my arm
I got up and closed all the windows
   And opened up my heart

Throw You Away

When it happened
You were all I wanted
All I wanted in the world
I wanted to collapse at your doorstep
In your arms
At your feet
I wanted to tell you all the things exploding inside me
The things that would never leave
The sound of my father's voice on the phone
The things he said
How long my mother and I stood in the hallway of her house
The things she said
How much we cried
And all I wanted was your voice
As night fell
And we traveled to her apartment
And I had to see my note
I had to see
And the hole that opened up inside me
When I saw it
That I didn't sign it with "love"
I didn't tell her I loved her
I knew I'd considered it
But I didn't do it
Just "- Ryan"
I wanted to beg you to tell me why
Why was it a consideration?
How much was my fault?
And please hold me in this world

But I didn't text you
I didn't call you
And everything I've ever named
Falling, crisis, nighttime, gone
The void, the nothing, breaking, me
Nothing compared
No words could save me
I didn't exist
And now time has passed
And what do we feel like?
And I hadn't thought about you until now
How important you seemed

Before all this
Yes, a certain amount of care was there
But that wasn't love
That wasn't fucking *love*
And now I wonder
If there could be
Any kind of love to rival
What I just couldn't write in that note
Because I would throw you away
Just to be able to go back
And tell her I love her

Ants

We sat in the empty Mexican restaurant
The three of us lost and alone together
The sign on the door said they were open to 50% capacity
And they were open for take-out
It was the first day of the Bay Area stay-at-home order
But we were 280 miles north
And only concerned that the orders would interfere
With the celebration of life

So the restaurant was empty
And we talked about nothing
And we thought about my sister
We thought about their daughter
And I talked about a poem I wrote about passing things down
The things we think we might have lost
The weight we have when we're gone
But mostly we talked about nothing

I kept finding ants on the side of my glass
Dead ants, as if they crawled onto the glass as it was
    drying
And then the drink was served, and no one noticed
I didn't notice the first one until we were almost done
And somehow I kept finding more
But if they were crawling from somewhere, I never saw it
I just picked each one off the glass
And dropped it in the crack between the seat and the wall
And I didn't bring it up
They'd had enough bad news
And right then, I didn't feel it was worth complaining
    about

Facebook Marketing

My organic reach tanked once I hit 10,000 likes
Thanks, Facebook
You almighty beacon of false hope
Tempting the naive architects of fledgling ventures
With slowly rising engagement
Waiting for the one time that they look up
And lick their lips in anticipation of the food-pellet
  morphine drip
The perfect moment to shut it all down
To turn the square-head valve on a demographic with no wrenches
That's what the numbers say
The numbers say "when"
And I don't fault the number machine
But loyalty begets loyalty
And the number machine can't look me in the eyes
And tell me it can't live without me
Tell me I make it proud
Thank me just for being there
It can't hold me like only a mother could
And tell me I was a good brother
No, the facsimile painted mask has the wrong expression
Those glaring eyes on the moth's wings
Don't trigger my genetic alarm mechanism
"He is not the demo," executives explain
Smoothing out the imperceptible dip in the upward trend
With the running of a finger across a scroll wheel

I am not the demo

Things Drawn Out by Mountain Sunsets

I can smell the trees on the air
The scent drawn out as the air cools
In the mountain sunset

The first hint of summer
And summer's what I need
What we *all* need

But I don't know if we'll quite get this one
As we set our minds on loving what's lost
And things drawn out by mountain sunsets

Listening to the Rain in the Dark

It's dark
I can barely see the lines of the page
As the first droplets of a late-spring rain
Pad down on the leaves outside
On the dirt, on the cement walkway separating apartments
Too light to hear them land on my rooftop
But not too light to hear them from the next rooftop over
And as gently as it began
The rain subsides

Now it's dark and silent
Leaving nothing to stop me from writing about
What I don't want to write about
How every human relationship I see these days
Real or fictional
Brothers, sisters, daughters, sons
Mothers, fathers, friends, and lovers
Brings me to the brink of tears
And if I'm all alone, I let that edge overflow
And I never want it to go away
I won't let it go away
Just how wonderful it is that we don't pass through
One another's lives
Without leaving an impression, a memory
Echoes of ourselves
The padding of the rain on the leaves between two
  apartments

I never just stopped to listen to the rain
Now, it's all I do
Because I know I'll never hear it again
Never that exact sound again
I bear witness to each and every drop
And let them carry me away into the dark

An Unbearable Lightness

It took so long to finish the book
Starting it was a holding on to her
And finishing it was the sign that she was gone
But so much more had left between those pages
I wondered how much of it was me
If any of it could return
And who I'd never see again

6am

At 6am the thunder wanted to speak of summer
But the rain wouldn't let go of the springtime chill
I lay in bed, not quite dreaming
I lay in bed until the air was still

She Wanted to Sing

She furrowed her brow
Aware that she did
She wanted to sing
But didn't know that she did

She'd always felt close
To something at night
But the song never came
It was only the night

She'd adopted a name
To fit how she felt
But the song never came
And it's all that she felt

She'd traveled away
To start a new life
But the song never came
And she thought about life

She'd colored her hair
It was dark and then light
But the song never came
And she cut off the light

So she stood on the couch
Aware that she did
She wanted to sing
But didn't know that she did

Momentary Darknesses

The rain fell down
And then there was the sun

Winding and Open

I let go of the handle and looked at my hand
Skin a little red from upper pad to fingertips
The blood rushing back in felt cold for a few seconds
Cold before warm, as the skin deepened in red
Some phenomenon like the nerves reawakening
Something I've read about but can't bring to mind
But I'm reminded just how wonderful it is
How wonderful it is sometimes to feel anything at all
And as we drive back down through the canyon
What I feel is wonder
At the blood returning to my fingertips
The flurry of warm air in this too-hot car
The four of us, right here and now
And just how much there is still left to feel

Acknowledgements

Thanks to everyone who got me here. Because I missed fully acknowledging the band in my last book--and shame on me for that--thanks to the rest of The Virals: Frank Wangberg, Jake Davis, and Zach Gibson. Without those days this book and the last wouldn't exist. Shout out to my brother Dillon too. He was there at the beginning of The Virals, and without him we wouldn't have had that name.

I have to acknowledge a few books that were influential in my life during the writing of this book: *Milk and Honey* by Rupi Kaur, *Bluets* by Maggie Nelson, *The Apple Trees at Olema: New and Selected Poems* by Robert Hass, *The Unbearable Lightness of Being* by Milan Kundera, and *A Field Guide to Getting Lost* by Rebecca Solnit. Without them, things would have been different.

Finally and most importantly, thank you to my family, to those who come together when things fall apart. Without them, the fall-apart is all there is.

--

Whether your family is biological, extended, or even just a group of friends, remember the part of that love that won't let go. And when you just can't hold on any longer,

let it catch you when you fall.

Ryan K. Allen
October 27, 2020

www.ingramcontent.com/pod-product-compliance
Lightning Source LLC
Chambersburg PA
CBHW022113040426
42450CB00006B/684